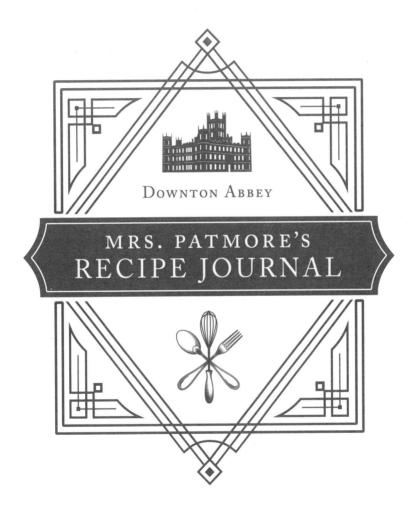

DOWNTON ABBEY

MRS. PATMORE'S
RECIPE JOURNAL

◇ RECIPE ◇

SERVES:

◈ INGREDIENTS ◈

◈ METHOD ◈

"Nothing in life is sure."

◇ RECIPE ◇

SERVES:

◇ INGREDIENTS ◇

◇ METHOD ◇

MRS. PATMORE

There is a man who's been shaken to the roots of his soul. Everything he based his life on has proved mortal after all.

MRS. HUGHES

We've no time for philosophy, Mrs. Patmore. What can we do to help?

MRS. PATMORE

Let's send up some coffee.

SEASON 6, EPISODE 5

◊ RECIPE ◊

SERVES:

◈ INGREDIENTS ◈

◈ METHOD ◈

> *"Oh why not just serve 'em bread and cheese then and have done with it?"*
>
> **MRS. PATMORE**
> SEASON 3, EPISODE 6

◇ RECIPE ◇

SERVES:

◇ INGREDIENTS ◇

◇ METHOD ◇

"There's nothing wrong with a man who can cook.
Some say the best cooks in the world are men."

MRS. PATMORE
SEASON 3, EPISODE 7

◇ RECIPE ◇

SERVES:

◈ INGREDIENTS ◈

◈ METHOD ◈

◇ RECIPE ◇

SERVES:

◇ INGREDIENTS ◇

◇ METHOD ◇

MRS. PATMORE

I've got tea for all of us, and a snack for you later on.

MASON

You're an angel of mercy.

SEASON 6, EPISODE 5

◇ RECIPE ◇

SERVES:

◆ INGREDIENTS ◆

◆ METHOD ◆

"*A bad workman always blames his tools.*"

MRS. PATMORE

SEASON 3, EPISODE 2

◇ RECIPE ◇

SERVES:

◇ INGREDIENTS ◇

◇ METHOD ◇

"He's very kind, you know. We should always be polite to people who are kind. There's not much of it about!"

MRS. PATMORE

SEASON 5, EPISODE 6

◇ RECIPE ◇

SERVES:

◇ INGREDIENTS ◇

◇ METHOD ◇

> *"Well, the cat's away, so we mice might as well play a little."*
>
> **MRS. PATMORE**
>
> SEASON 5, EPISODE 9

◇ RECIPE ◇

SERVES:

◈ INGREDIENTS ◈

◈ METHOD ◈

◇ RECIPE ◇

SERVES:

◇ INGREDIENTS ◇

◇ METHOD ◇

"*Oh, well, of course, as we all know, anyone can cook.*"

MRS. PATMORE

SEASON 6, EPISODE 5

◇ RECIPE ◇

SERVES:

◇ INGREDIENTS ◇

◇ METHOD ◇

"It's that bloomin' Daisy! I've said she'll be the death of me, and now my word's come true!"

◇ RECIPE ◇

SERVES:

◈ INGREDIENTS ◈

◈ METHOD ◈

> *"No, don't stop stirring, the bottom will burn!"*

MRS. PATMORE

SEASON 2, EPISODE 4

◇ RECIPE ◇

SERVES:

◈ INGREDIENTS ◈

◈ METHOD ◈

DAISY

I was only trying to help.

MRS. PATMORE

Oh like Judas was only "trying to help," I s'pose, when he brought the Roman soldiers to the garden!

SEASON 1, EPISODE 5

◇ RECIPE ◇

SERVES:

◈ INGREDIENTS ◈

◈ METHOD ◈

> *"Be off with you, you cheeky devil. Go on!"*

MRS. PATMORE

SEASON 3, EPISODE 9

RECIPE ⬦ ⬦

SERVES:

⬦⬦ INGREDIENTS ⬦⬦

⬦⬦ METHOD ⬦⬦

"I know the popular fantasy is that you can feed six strong men from a single seed cake, but you and I know better."

MRS. PATMORE

SEASON 2, EPISODE 3

◇ **RECIPE** ◇

SERVES:

◇ INGREDIENTS ◇

◇ METHOD ◇

"*Never mind that. At times like these, we must all pull together.*"

MRS. PATMORE

SEASON 2, EPISODE 8

◇ RECIPE ◇

SERVES:

◈ INGREDIENTS ◈

◈ METHOD ◈

DAISY

A penny for your thoughts.

MRS. PATMORE

They're worth a great deal more than that, thank you very much.

SEASON 2, EPISODE 2

◇ RECIPE ◇

SERVES:

◇ INGREDIENTS ◇

◇ METHOD ◇

"Now, what else can I give you?
Another cup of tea, why not?"

◇ RECIPE ◇

SERVES:

◇ INGREDIENTS ◇

◇ METHOD ◇

"Ooh talk about making a silk purse out of a sow's ear.
I wish we had a sow's ear. It'd be better than this brisket."

MRS. PATMORE

SEASON 2, EPISODE 7

RECIPE

SERVES:

INGREDIENTS

METHOD

*"Daisy? Did you hear
me call? Or have you gone
selectively deaf?"*

MRS. PATMORE

SEASON I, EPISODE 2

◇ RECIPE ◇

SERVES:

◇ INGREDIENTS ◇

◇ METHOD ◇

SYBIL

Do you think it's ready?

MRS. PATMORE

I know it's ready.

SEASON 2, EPISODE I

◇ RECIPE ◇

SERVES:

◈ INGREDIENTS ◈

◈ METHOD ◈

*"Ooh my, my, will
wonders never cease?"*

MRS. PATMORE

SEASON I, EPISODE I

◇ RECIPE ◇

SERVES:

◈ INGREDIENTS ◈

◈ METHOD ◈

"Oh, I'll have no swear words in here, thank you very much. Unless I'm doing the swearing."

MRS. PATMORE

SEASON 4, EPISODE 3

◇ RECIPE ◇

SERVES:

◇ INGREDIENTS ◇

◇ METHOD ◇

*"What's this? Do I hear
my name taken in vain?"*

MRS. PATMORE

SEASON 3, EPISODE 9

◇ RECIPE ◇

SERVES:

◇ INGREDIENTS ◇

◇ METHOD ◇

MRS. PATMORE

*But you can't manage a broth,
Miss Denker, special or otherwise?*

DENKER

*Well, of course I would be
very good at it -*

MRS. PATMORE

If you only knew where to start.

◇ RECIPE ◇

SERVES:

◈ INGREDIENTS ◈

◈ METHOD ◈

*"Oh! You couldn't be harder
on those potatoes if you wanted
them to confess to spying."*

MRS. PATMORE

SEASON 6, EPISODE 4

◇ RECIPE ◇

SERVES:

◇ INGREDIENTS ◇

◇ METHOD ◇

*"Use an alarm clock to remind you when to put things
in the oven and when to take them out."*

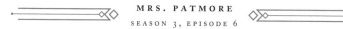

MRS. PATMORE
SEASON 3, EPISODE 6

◇ RECIPE ◇

SERVES:

◇ INGREDIENTS ◇

◇ METHOD ◇

> *"Fold it in, don't slap it!*
> *You're making a cake, not*
> *beating a carpet!"*

MRS. PATMORE
SEASON 2, EPISODE 2

◇ RECIPE ◇

SERVES:

◇ INGREDIENTS ◇

◇ METHOD ◇

DAISY

It's a mixer. It beats eggs and whips cream and all sorts.

MRS. PATMORE

But you and Ivy do that.

DAISY

And we'd be glad not to, thank you very much.

SEASON 4, EPISODE I

◇ RECIPE ◇

SERVES:

◇ INGREDIENTS ◇

◇ METHOD ◇

*"If it's all right with you,
I've to tackle tonight's dinner."*

MRS. PATMORE

SEASON 5, EPISODE 1

◇ RECIPE ◇

SERVES:

◇ INGREDIENTS ◇

◇ METHOD ◇

*"Listen to me! And get those kidneys up to the servery
before I knock you down and serve your brains as fritters."*

MRS. PATMORE

SEASON 1, EPISODE 2

◇ RECIPE ◇

SERVES:

◇ INGREDIENTS ◇

◇ METHOD ◇

"Yes. Well. Sympathy butters no parsnips. I'd better get on."

MRS. PATMORE
SEASON 5, EPISODE 3

◇ RECIPE ◇

SERVES:

◇◇ INGREDIENTS ◇◇

◇◇ METHOD ◇◇

◇ RECIPE ◇

SERVES:

◈ INGREDIENTS ◈

◈ METHOD ◈

"This stuff is thirsty work."

MRS. PATMORE

SEASON 2, EPISODE 9

◇ RECIPE ◇

SERVES:

◇ INGREDIENTS ◇

◇ METHOD ◇

"There's lobster rissoles in Mousseline sauce or Calvados-glazed duckling, or do you fancy a little asparagus salad with Champagne-saffron vinaigrette?"

MRS. PATMORE

SEASON 3, EPISODE 3

◇ RECIPE ◇

SERVES:

◆ INGREDIENTS ◆

◆ METHOD ◆

*"I had to get out of that
kitchen if I'm not to be found
dead under the table."*

MRS. PATMORE

SEASON 2, EPISODE 4

◇ RECIPE ◇

SERVES:

◈ INGREDIENTS ◈

◈ METHOD ◈

MRS. PATMORE

I know it's cheating but I think I might get a jar of horseradish. It really isn't bad now.

DAISY

That's not like you.

SEASON 6, EPISODE 2

◇ RECIPE ◇

SERVES:

◇ INGREDIENTS ◇

◇ METHOD ◇

> *"Anyone who has the use of their limbs can make a salmon mousse."*

MRS. PATMORE
SEASON 3, EPISODE 6

◇ RECIPE ◇

SERVES:

◆ INGREDIENTS ◆

◆ METHOD ◆

*"Now steady. Even the most experienced cook can
burn themself if they're not careful."*

◇ RECIPE ◇

SERVES:

◈ INGREDIENTS ◈

◈ METHOD ◈

*"Oh I'm not just
a pretty face."*

MRS. PATMORE

SEASON 3, EPISODE 9

SERVES:

◈ **INGREDIENTS** ◈

◈ **METHOD** ◈

◇ RECIPE ◇

SERVES:

◈ INGREDIENTS ◈

◈ METHOD ◈

"Now go and grate that suet
before I grow old and die."

MRS. PATMORE

SEASON 2, EPISODE 3

◇ RECIPE ◇

SERVES:

◇ INGREDIENTS ◇

◇ METHOD ◇

"Nothing's as changeable as a young man's heart.
Take hope and a warning from that."

MRS. PATMORE

◇ RECIPE ◇

SERVES:

◈ INGREDIENTS ◈

◈ METHOD ◈

"*Have a bit of the tart
if you like.*"

MRS. PATMORE

SEASON 3, EPISODE 9

◇ RECIPE ◇

SERVES:

◇ INGREDIENTS ◇

◇ METHOD ◇

◇ RECIPE ◇

SERVES:

◇ INGREDIENTS ◇

◇ METHOD ◇

"Get away with you,
you daft beggar!"

MRS. PATMORE

SEASON 3, EPISODE 9

◇ RECIPE ◇

SERVES:

◈ INGREDIENTS ◈

◈ METHOD ◈

"The more he said about how he liked his beef roasted and his eggs fried
and his pancakes flipped, the more I wondered how to get away."

MRS. PATMORE

SEASON 3, EPISODE 9

◇ RECIPE ◇

SERVES:

◇ INGREDIENTS ◇

◇ METHOD ◇

"Would you mind taking the
coffee up while it's still hot?
Or is that too much to ask?"

MRS. PATMORE
SEASON 5, EPISODE 8

◇ RECIPE ◇

SERVES:

◈ INGREDIENTS ◈

◈ METHOD ◈

GEORGE

Can I lick the bowl?

MRS. PATMORE

Yes. You can both lick the bowl.

SEASON 6, EPISODE 1

◇ RECIPE ◇

SERVES:

◇ INGREDIENTS ◇

◇ METHOD ◇

"Well they've not turned out so badly, have they?"

MRS. PATMORE

SEASON 5, EPISODE 2

◇ RECIPE ◇

SERVES:

◈ INGREDIENTS ◈

◈ METHOD ◈

"I'd love to think I had a secret that was too indelicate
for a lady's ear, but I haven't."

MRS. PATMORE

SEASON 5, EPISODE 5

◇ **RECIPE** ◇

SERVES:

◈ **INGREDIENTS** ◈

◈ **METHOD** ◈

> *"Oh, dear. We're not having another crisis, are we?"*

MRS. PATMORE

SEASON 5, EPISODE 9

◇ RECIPE ◇

SERVES:

◇ INGREDIENTS ◇

◇ METHOD ◇

MOLESLEY

Can I borrow some soda,
Mrs Patmore?

MRS. PATMORE

Borrow? So you'll give it back?

SEASON 6, EPISODE 2

◇ RECIPE ◇

SERVES:

◇◇ INGREDIENTS ◇◇

◇◇ METHOD ◇◇

"I'll crown you if you don't get that back on the heat."

MRS. PATMORE

◇ RECIPE ◇

SERVES:

◇ INGREDIENTS ◇

◇ METHOD ◇

"*We should celebrate. Come into the kitchen while I get the dinner going. There's a bottle of wine there and Mr. Carson wouldn't mind.*"

MRS. PATMORE

SEASON 6, EPISODE 7

◇ RECIPE ◇

SERVES:

◇ INGREDIENTS ◇

◇ METHOD ◇

*"You're not a quick
learner, are you?"*

MRS. PATMORE

SEASON 6, EPISODE 2

◇ RECIPE ◇

SERVES:

◈ INGREDIENTS ◈

◈ METHOD ◈

DAISY

I can't believe Miss O'Brien would be so thoughtless.

MRS. PATMORE

Can't you? I can.

SEASON 4, EPISODE 1

◇ **RECIPE** ◇

SERVES:

◈ INGREDIENTS ◈

◈ METHOD ◈

> *"It never does good*
> *to hate anyone."*
>
> **MRS. PATMORE**
> SEASON 6, EPISODE 4

SERVES:

◇ **INGREDIENTS** ◇

◇ **METHOD** ◇

"I'm crying because I don't want you to leave. I'll miss you. Don't, don't concern yourself. I'll get over it."

MRS. PATMORE
SEASON 5, EPISODE 8

◇ RECIPE ◇

SERVES:

◈ INGREDIENTS ◈

◈ METHOD ◈

"What the eye can't see,
the heart won't grieve over."

MRS. PATMORE

SEASON I, EPISODE 5

◇ RECIPE ◇

SERVES:

◈ INGREDIENTS ◈

◈ METHOD ◈

MRS. PATMORE

*Now spoon it into the shells.
No not like that! Oh, give it here!*

DAISY

Mrs Patmore, we can do this.

MRS. PATMORE

*Oh can you? With Ivy slapping
it out like a trained seal.*

SEASON 4, EPISODE 3

◇ RECIPE ◇

SERVES:

◈ INGREDIENTS ◈

◈ METHOD ◈

"I cannot work from a new receipt at a moment's notice!"

MRS. PATMORE

SEASON I, EPISODE 5

◇ RECIPE ◇

SERVES:

◈ INGREDIENTS ◈

◈ METHOD ◈

_"Oh not those bowls, Ivy! Chilled soup should be an
exquisite mouthful, not a bucket of slop!"_

MRS. PATMORE
SEASON 4, EPISODE 3

NOTES

NOTES

NOTES

NOTES

NOTES

NOTES

NOTES

RECIPE   COURSE   PAGE

RECIPE	COURSE	PAGE

RECIPE   COURSE   PAGE

RECIPE	COURSE	PAGE

KITCHEN MEASUREMENTS

CUP	TBSP	TSP	FL OZ
1/16 CUP	1 TBSP	3 TSP	1/2 FLOZ
1/8 CUP	2 TBSP	6 TSP	1 FLOZ
1/4 CUP	4 TBSP	12 TSP	2 FLOZ
1/3 CUP	5 1/3 TBSP	16 TSP	2 2/3 FLOZ
1/2 CUP	8 TBSP	24 TSP	4 FLOZ
2/3 CUP	10 2/3 TBSP	32 TSP	5 1/3 FLOZ
3/4 CUP	12 TBSP	36 TSP	6 FLOZ
1 CUP	16 TBSP	48 TSP	8 FLOZ

GALLON	QUART	PINT	CUP	FL OZ
1/16 GAL	1/4 QT	1/2 PINTS	1 CUP	8 FLOZ
1/8 GAL	1/2 QT	1 PINTS	2 CUP	16 FLOZ
1/4 GAL	1 QT	2 PINTS	4 CUP	32 FLOZ
1/2 GAL	2 QT	4 PINTS	8 CUP	64 FLOZ
1 GAL	4 QT	8 PINTS	16 CUP	128 FLOZ

weldon**owen**

Printed and bound in China
First published in 2021

10 9 8 7 6 5 4 3 2 1

WEIGHT

GRAMS	OUNCE
14 g	½ oz
28 g	1 oz
57 g	2 oz
85 g	3 oz
113 g	4 oz
142 g	5 oz
170 g	6 oz
283 g	10 oz
397 g	14 oz
454 g	16 oz
907 g	32 oz

OVEN TEMPERATURES

CELSIUS	FAHRENHEIT
93°C	200°F
107°C	225°F
121°C	250°F
135°C	275°F
149°C	300°F
163°C	325°F
177°C	350°F
191°C	375°F
204°C	400°F
218°C	425°F
232°C	450°F

LENGTH

METRIC	2.5 cm	5 cm	10 cm	15 cm	20 cm	25 cm	30 cm
IMPERIAL	1 in	2 in	4 in	6 in	8 in	10 in	12 in